sauces

sauces

louise pickford

photography by **ian wallace**

RYLAND
PETERS
& SMALL

LONDON NEW YORK

First published in the
United Kingdom in 2007
by Ryland Peters & Small
20–21 Jockey's Fields
London WC1R 4BW
www.rylandpeters.com

10 9 8 7 6 5 4 3 2 1

ISBN 978 1 84597 482 4

A CIP record for this book is available
from the British Library.

Printed in China

Editor   **Céline Hughes**
Production   **Gordana Simakovic**
Publishing Director   **Alison Starling**

Stylist   **Louise Pickford**
Prop merchandiser   **David Morgan**
Indexer   **Hilary Bird**

Notes

• All spoon measurements are level, unless
otherwise specified.

• All eggs are medium, unless otherwise
specified. Recipes containing raw or partially
cooked egg, or raw fish or shellfish, should not
be served to the very young, very old, anyone
with a compromised immune system or
pregnant women.

• To sterilize bottles and jars, wash well in
soapy water, rinse thoroughly, then boil in
plenty of water for 10 minutes. Using tongs,
remove the bottles or jars from the water. They
should be filled as soon as they are dry, and
still hot. If the sauce is cold, leave the bottle
or jar to cool before filling.

Author's acknowledgements

I would like to thank my husband Ian for his
beautiful photography – I think this is some of
his best work – and of course for being my
number one recipe tester and harshest critic!
Thanks to David Morgan for his exquisite taste
in props. Thanks to Jennifer Tolhurst for
assisting me on the food shoot – as always she
was a joy to work with. All of the above have
helped me create this special book. All my
thanks too to Alison, Paul, Ann and Céline at
RPS for all their work and continued support.

A big thank you also to the following shops in
Sydney for the loan of props:

Mud Australia (www.mudaustralia.com)

Papaya (www.papaya.com.au)

Simon Johnson (www.simonjohnson.com.au)

Aeria Country Floors

CONTENTS

INTRODUCTION

Sauces can be divided into two main categories: those that accompany the principal ingredient of a dish and those that form the basis, as in a stew. This book concentrates on the former and offers a wide variety of sauces ranging from the classic French sauces and emulsions to more rustic Italian-style salsas, Asian dipping sauces, dressings and sweet sauces. All the basic stocks are covered and whilst some recipes will be familiar, many provide a new twist to an old favourite as well as offering new and exciting ideas too.

If you look at the history of sauces and sauce-making, a large proportion are French in origin, and although some can be traced back several hundred years, many are based on those invented in the late nineteenth and early twentieth centuries by such famous French chefs as Carême and Escoffier. These are the more classic sauces, such as béchamel, velouté, glace, mayonnaise and hollandaise, to name but a few. Today the definition of 'sauce' is far wider-reaching. Think of the herb salsas of Italy, nut sauces of North Africa, fiery dipping sauces of Southeast Asia and salad dressings from every corner of the earth. Flavoured oils, vinegars and marinades all have a role to play too and are often the base for a finished sauce.

Whatever type of sauce you make, its main purpose is to enhance the principal ingredient it is served with, not to overpower it in any way. The recipes in this book are divided into those

that traditionally partner meat, fish, pasta and vegetables so they can be readily located, but there are no hard-and-fast rules. My serving suggestions are exactly that – a personal preference, and it's up to you to choose the type of sauce you want to serve with what. When it comes to seasoning, this too must be a personal choice; I can only advise according to my taste buds, so always taste, taste and taste again as you cook, then you will be able to add a little more salt and pepper if you want it.

TYPES OF SAUCES

Thickened sauces A roux is a thickened sauce made with an equal amount of butter and flour that are cooked together before a liquid is added. As the mixture boils, the sauce thickens. The most common roux sauce is Béchamel (see page 16).

A beurre manié is also made with equal quantities of flour and butter but this time the mixture is whisked raw into the sauce towards the end of cooking. The sauce thickens as it returns to the boil. This method is more commonly used in braised dishes and stews.

Other last-minute thickeners like cornflour are widely used in Chinese cooking, to give the finished sauce viscosity. Egg yolks and cream are also whisked into some sauces at the end of cooking, serving to both thicken the sauce and enrich it.

Reduced sauces Stocks and other liquids are often reduced by boiling, which not only thickens the sauce, but also concentrates the flavour. This method is adopted mainly in professional kitchens, where huge pots of stock are reduced down until they are transformed to a rich glaze, such as Meat Glaze (or Glace, see page 10).

Emulsions This is a sauce formed when two very different ingredients, a water-based liquid and an oil or fat, are whisked vigorously to form a smooth sauce, which is stabilized by the addition of egg yolks. Examples include Mayonnaise (see page 20), which is a cold egg sauce made by whisking oil into a base of egg yolks, vinegar (or lemon juice) and mustard, and Hollandaise (see page 18) which is a hot egg sauce made by whisking egg yolks over heat to help thicken and stabilize them.

A simplified emulsion is Beurre Blanc (see page 77), a butter sauce made by whisking butter into a reduction of vinegar (or lemon juice). Here the absence of egg yolks makes it the most delicate emulsion. Beurre blanc is always served tepid because it splits if it is too hot.

Puréed sauces Vegetables and fruits are perfect for puréeing to give an immediate and fresh tasting sauce like Melba Sauce (see page 92). Sauces such as the Italian Salsa Verde (see page 32) and Green Curry Paste (see page 40) are types of puréed sauces too and these were traditionally pounded using a pestle and mortar.

Enriched sauces Butter is used to add extra richness to some sauces, especially meat sauces, and this is called 'mounting' a sauce. Just before serving, the pan is removed from the heat (or kept on a very low heat) and a small amount of chilled, unsalted butter is gradually incorporated by swirling the pan gently, allowing the butter to melt into the sauce until glossy.

EQUIPMENT

You need very little specialist equipment to make sauces. Here are the essentials:

Saucepans and stockpots A good range of different sized pans is important, beginning with a large, aluminium stockpot (3.6-litre capacity). For the rest of your saucepans, buy the best you can afford – stainless steel pans with a thick layer of copper in the base are perfect because copper is an excellent heat conductor. A milk saucepan with a lip for pouring finished sauces directly onto plates is very useful.

Sieves Use a large, wide sieve for straining sauces at the beginning of cooking, and a fine, conical sieve for straining finished sauces – this gives the sauce a nice shine.

Whisks You should have at least one balloon whisk and an electric whisk for beating in large quantities of oil or butter.

Wooden spoons The thickness of some sauces is measured by the way they coat the back of a wooden spoon (see page 88). Buy a selection for sweet and savoury sauces and try to keep them separate as they can become discoloured.

Measuring jugs Buy a selection of sizes, from 500-ml jugs to larger ones with at least a 2-litre capacity.

Scales Every kitchen should have a good set of weighing scales – electronic ones are the most accurate.

Food processor This is essential for puréeing sauces and making pastes and dips.

Spice grinder This is useful but not essential, and a coffee grinder will suffice.

Pestle and mortar These can be used in place of a spice or coffee grinder. They are relatively inexpensive and will last a lifetime.

INGREDIENTS

Butter It is best to use unsalted butter or one with reduced salt in all sauces – it gives a better result and allows you to control the level of salt in your cooking.

Eggs Use free-range eggs whenever possible and always check the expiry date so that you use the freshest eggs available. If you store eggs in the fridge, return them to room temperature 1 hour before using.

Cream Double cream is best for sauces as it is the most stable and can be boiled and reduced without breaking down. Crème fraîche can also be used in the same way. You can also use single or whipping cream, but be careful not to allow either to split.

Salt and pepper Use sea salt and freshly ground black peppercorns.

Bouquet garni This is a useful addition to stocks. Wrap in muslin instead of leek skin, if preferred.

a 7.5-cm length of leek
a 7.5-cm length of celery stick
1 garlic clove, peeled
2 fresh bay leaves (or 1 dried)
2 fresh flat leaf parsley sprigs
2 fresh thyme sprigs
6 black peppercorns

Remove the outer layer of leek (reserving the rest for the stock) and open out flat. Put the remaining ingredients on top of the leek skin (or on a piece of muslin), then roll up tightly. Tie up with kitchen string.

CLASSICS

BEEF STOCK

A deeply flavoured beef stock will make all the difference to a finished sauce. Beef blade is available on or off the bone, but for a particularly flavoursome stock, buy it on the bone.

4 tablespoons extra virgin olive oil
2 kg beef blade, cut into chunks
3 large onions, chopped
4 carrots, chopped
4 celery sticks, chopped
1 Bouquet Garni *(page 7)*
2 teaspoons sea salt

MAKES: APPROXIMATELY 2 LITRES

[1] Heat the olive oil in a large stockpot and fry the beef blade in several batches until well browned.

[2] Add the remaining ingredients and 4 litres cold water and bring slowly to the boil, skimming the surface to remove the scum. Partially cover the pan and simmer gently for 3–4 hours until the stock is reduced by half and full of flavour. Season to taste.

[3] Strain the stock through a fine sieve and leave to cool, then refrigerate for up to 3 days.

[4] When you are ready to use the stock, remove the thick layer of fat from the surface.

VARIATION: **MEAT GLAZE (GLACE)**

Return the strained stock to a clean pan and simmer until reduced to approximately 300 ml. Leave to cool. Refrigerate for up to 1 month.

CHICKEN STOCK

a 2-kg chicken, washed
2 onions, chopped
2 carrots, chopped
2 celery sticks, chopped
2 leeks, chopped
2 garlic cloves, peeled
1 Bouquet Garni *(page 7)*
2 teaspoons sea salt

MAKES: APPROXIMATELY 2 LITRES

Refrigerating the cold stock overnight allows the fat to solidify on the surface of the stock, making it much easier to remove.

Put the chicken in a large stockpot with all the remaining ingredients and cover with cold water (about 2 litres).

Bring slowly to the boil, skimming the surface to remove the scum. Partially cover the pan and simmer gently for 3 hours. Strain the stock through a fine sieve and leave to cool, then refrigerate overnight.

Remove the thick layer of fat from the surface. Refrigerate for up to 3 days.

BEEF STOCK

FISH STOCK

1 kg fish trimmings
a 750-ml bottle dry white wine
1 tablespoon white wine vinegar
2 large carrots, chopped
1 onion, chopped
2 celery sticks, chopped
1 leek, chopped
2 garlic cloves, peeled
1 Bouquet Garni *(page 7)*
1 teaspoon sea salt

MAKES: APPROXIMATELY 1.25 LITRES

The important factor when making fish stock is to simmer the fish trimmings for only 30 minutes, especially if the heads are used, otherwise it becomes bitter. Most fishmongers will happily give you their fish trimmings.

Wash the fish trimmings and put in a large saucepan with all the remaining ingredients and 1.5 litres cold water. Bring to the boil, skimming the surface to remove the scum. Partially cover the pan and simmer gently for 30 minutes.

Strain the stock through a fine sieve into a clean pan and return to the boil. Simmer, uncovered, for 15 minutes, or until the liquid is reduced by half. You should be left with approximately 1.25 litres fish stock. Leave to cool and refrigerate for up to 3 days.

VEGETABLE STOCK

Extracting the maximum flavour from your stock is vital, especially in a vegetable stock. The addition of the lentils adds an earthy flavour; brown rice can be used as an alternative.

2 tablespoons extra virgin olive oil
2 garlic cloves, peeled
1 onion, roughly chopped
1 large leek, chopped
2 carrots, chopped
2 potatoes, cubed
2 celery sticks, chopped
150 ml dry white wine
1 ripe tomato, chopped
125 g mushrooms, chopped
50 g red lentils
1 Bouquet Garni *(page 7)*
2 teaspoons sea salt

MAKES: APPROXIMATELY 1.75 LITRES

Heat the olive oil in a large saucepan and fry the garlic, onion and leek for 10 minutes. Add the carrots, potatoes and celery and fry for a further 10 minutes, or until softened but not coloured.

Add the wine and boil rapidly for 2–3 minutes, or until almost completely reduced. Add the remaining ingredients and 1.75 litres cold water and bring to the boil. Cover and simmer for 1 hour.

Strain the stock through a fine sieve and leave to cool completely. Refrigerate for up to 3 days.

PAN-FRIED LAMB CUTLETS WITH BROWN SAUCE, WILTED SPINACH
AND OVEN-ROASTED CHERRY TOMATOES

BROWN SAUCE

Brown sauce, or *espagnole*, is French in origin and dates back to the eighteenth century. The rather lengthy original version has been simplified over the years to a more basic brown roux. It is traditionally served with red meat, such as lamb or beef.

50 g smoked bacon, diced
25 g unsalted butter
2 shallots, finely chopped
1 carrot, finely chopped
100 g mushrooms, finely chopped
2 tablespoons plain flour
600 ml Beef Stock *(page 10)*
1 Bouquet Garni *(page 7)*
2 tablespoons tomato purée
1 tablespoon dry sherry
sea salt and freshly ground black pepper

MAKES: APPROXIMATELY 300 ML

Heat a saucepan and stir-fry the bacon for 3–4 minutes, or until browned and the fat has rendered into the pan. Add the butter and fry the shallots, carrot and mushrooms over medium heat for 8–10 minutes, or until the vegetables are evenly browned.

Stir the flour into the pan and cook for 2 minutes. Remove the pan from the heat and gradually stir in the beef stock until smooth. Return the pan to the heat and bring the sauce slowly to the boil, stirring constantly. Add the bouquet garni, tomato purée and seasoning, partially cover the pan and simmer very gently for 50–60 minutes, skimming the surface occasionally to remove the scum.

Strain the sauce through a fine sieve into a clean saucepan, add the sherry and heat through. Serve hot or cool. To store, cover the surface of the hot sauce with clingfilm, leave to cool and refrigerate for up to 3 days.

DEMI-GLACE

This type of rich, intensely flavoured stock is typical of those made in restaurant kitchens, but it can easily be made at home for a truly delicious sauce to accompany red meat, especially pan-fried fillet steak.

1 quantity Brown Sauce *(see above)*
25 g mushrooms, finely chopped
1 teaspoon tomato purée
2 tablespoons Meat Glaze *(page 10)*
1 tablespoon Madeira
15 g unsalted butter, chilled and diced

MAKES: APPROXIMATELY 250 ML

Put the brown sauce, mushrooms, tomato purée, meat glaze and Madeira in a saucepan and heat gently until boiling. Simmer for 5 minutes, or until the liquid is reduced to about 250 ml. Remove the pan from the heat and whisk in the butter a little at a time until the sauce is glossy. Strain through a fine sieve and serve with pan-fried steak.

BECHAMEL SAUCE

Béchamel is a classic white roux sauce: butter and flour are cooked gently until they turn light golden, then scalded milk is whisked in. This creamy sauce forms the basis of many dishes, including lasagne, but is rarely served as a sauce in itself. This makes enough for a lasagne serving 6–8 people.

2 onions, roughly chopped
4 fresh bay leaves
4 whole cloves
1.2 litres milk

80 g unsalted butter
80 g plain flour
sea salt and freshly ground black pepper

MAKES: APPROXIMATELY 1.2 LITRES

Put the onions, bay leaves, cloves, milk and seasoning into a saucepan, bring to the boil and immediately remove from the heat. Set aside to infuse for 20 minutes, then strain.

To make the roux, melt the butter in a clean saucepan, add the flour and cook over medium heat, stirring, for 1 minute. Gradually stir in the strained milk and continue to cook, stirring, until the mixture boils. Simmer for 2 minutes and remove from the heat.

VARIATION: **MORNAY SAUCE**

1 quantity Béchamel Sauce *(see above)*
200 g grated Cheddar or other cheese

Heat the béchamel sauce and stir in the Cheddar until melted. Serve hot.

VELOUTE SAUCE

Velouté, meaning 'velvety' in French, is another roux-based sauce but this time made with stock. The roux is cooked until golden, then stock is added and the sauce is simmered until reduced. Egg yolks or cream are stirred in to further enrich the velouté. It is often served with chicken dishes.

500 ml Chicken Stock *(page 10)*
25 g unsalted butter
25 g plain flour
50 ml double cream

MAKES: APPROXIMATELY 300 ML

Put the stock in a saucepan and bring to a gentle simmer. Meanwhile, melt the butter in another saucepan and stir in the flour. Cook over low heat for 2–3 minutes, or until golden. Remove the pan from the heat and whisk in the hot stock until combined.

Return the pan to the heat and bring to the boil, whisking constantly until the sauce thickens. Simmer gently for at least 20 minutes, skimming the surface from time to time. When the sauce is glossy, stir in the cream and warm through without letting it come to the boil. Serve hot.

BECHAMEL SAUCE

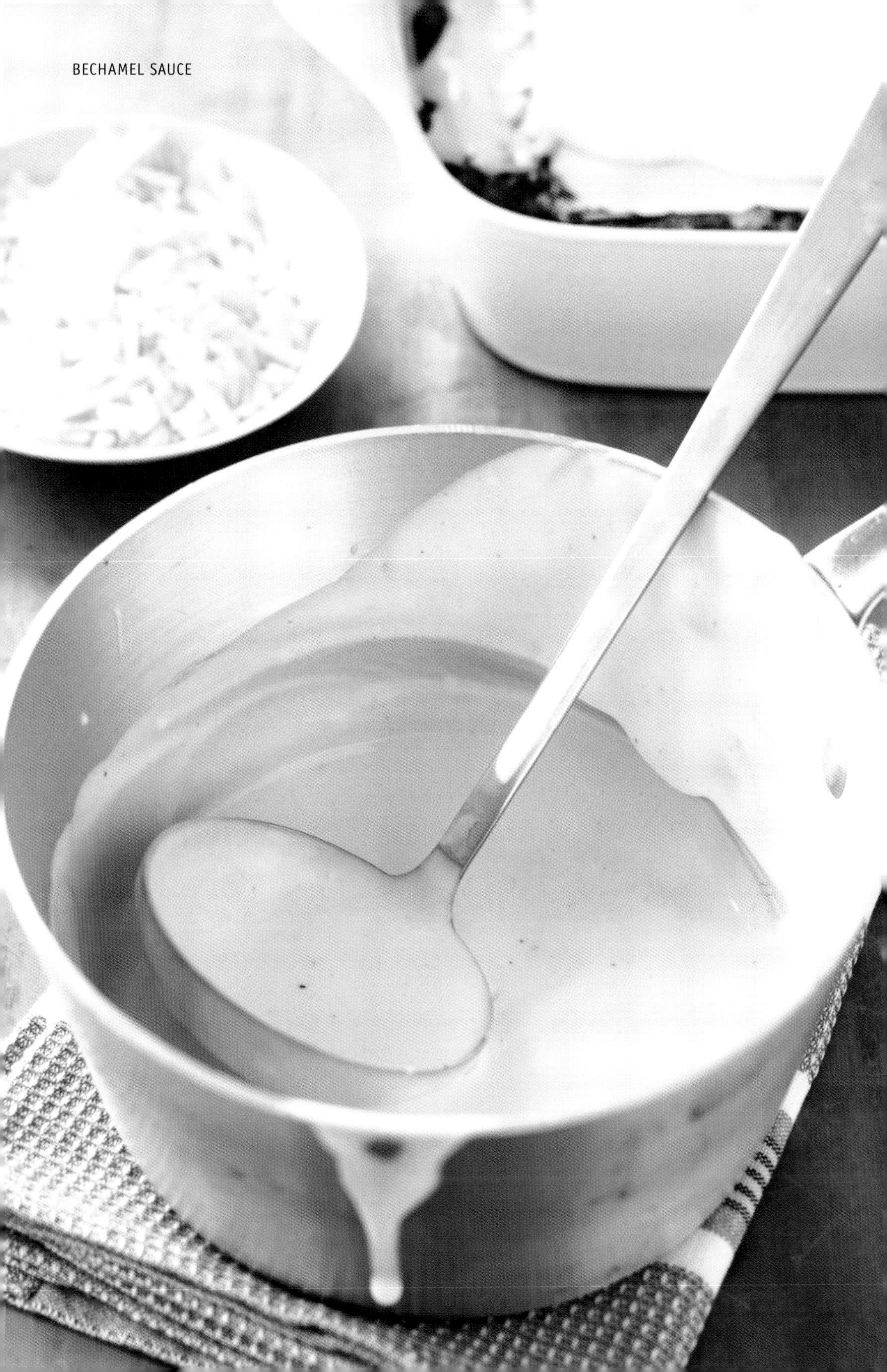

1 2 3

HOLLANDAISE SAUCE

Hollandaise is a smooth emulsion of butter, vinegar and eggs. Rich and velvety, this sauce is pure heaven when partnered with asparagus, artichokes or poached salmon.

150 g unsalted butter
2 tablespoons white wine vinegar
1 shallot, finely chopped
a pinch of sea salt
2 egg yolks

MAKES: APPROXIMATELY 200 ML

[1] Melt the butter very gently in a small saucepan. Pour it into a small jug through a muslin-lined tea strainer to remove any excess milk solids.

[2] Put the vinegar, shallot, salt and 1 tablespoon water in a small saucepan and heat gently until the liquid is almost totally evaporated, leaving only about 1 tablespoon. Remove from the heat and strain into a glass bowl.

[3] Place the bowl over a saucepan of gently simmering water (do not let the bowl touch the water). Add the egg yolks and, using a balloon whisk, whisk the mixture for 2 minutes, or until pale and frothy. Remove from the heat.

[4] Using an electric whisk, whisk in the melted butter, pouring it in in a slow, steady stream. Continue whisking until the sauce becomes thick and velvety. Serve warm.

VARIATION: **BEARNAISE SAUCE**

Aromatic tarragon added to the basic hollandaise emulsion creates a classic sauce popularly served with pan-fried steak and frites.

2 tablespoons tarragon vinegar
1 fresh tarragon sprig
1 tablespoon chopped fresh tarragon

MAKES: APPROXIMATELY 200 ML

Follow the method above for Hollandaise Sauce, but replace the white wine vinegar with the tarragon vinegar and add the tarragon sprig whilst reducing. Stir the chopped tarragon into the finished sauce.

4

3 egg yolks
2 teaspoons white
wine vinegar
1 teaspoon Dijon mustard
300 ml olive oil
sea salt and freshly
ground white pepper

MAKES: APPROXIMATELY 300 ML

MAYONNAISE

Mayonnaise is an emulsion of oil and vinegar with the addition of egg yolks to stabilize it. I prefer to use a milder, pure olive oil as extra virgin olive oil can be overly harsh and bitter.

Put the egg yolks, vinegar, mustard and a little seasoning in a bowl. Using an electric whisk, whisk until the mixture is frothy. Very gradually whisk in the olive oil, a little at a time, mixing well after each addition until the sauce is thick and glossy and all the oil is incorporated. Cover the surface of the sauce with clingfilm and refrigerate for up to 3 days.

Note: If the mayonnaise is too thick, then slowly whisk in 1–2 tablespoons boiling water to thin the sauce.

VARIATION: **AIOLI**

2–4 garlic cloves, peeled and crushed

Put the garlic in the bowl with the egg yolks, vinegar, mustard and seasoning, and continue to follow the recipe.

SESAME AND LIME MAYONNAISE

The sesame oil and seeds add a distinctly exotic flavour to mayonnaise. Serve with a platter of steamed or fresh green vegetables.

1 tablespoon sesame seeds
1 garlic clove, peeled
3 egg yolks
4 teaspoons freshly
squeezed lime juice
250 ml olive oil
2 teaspoons toasted
sesame oil
sea salt and freshly
ground black pepper

MAKES: APPROXIMATELY 250 ML

Put the sesame seeds and garlic in a mortar with a good pinch of salt and pound to form a smooth paste. Transfer to a bowl and add the egg yolks, lime juice and a little pepper.

Using an electric whisk, whisk until the mixture is frothy. Very gradually whisk in the olive oil, a little at a time, mixing well after each addition until the sauce is thick and glossy and all the oil is incorporated. Whisk in the sesame oil and season to taste.

TOP: MAYONNAISE
MIDDLE: AIOLI
BOTTOM: SESAME AND LIME MAYONNAISE

LEFT: HERB BUTTER
RIGHT: SAFFRON BUTTER

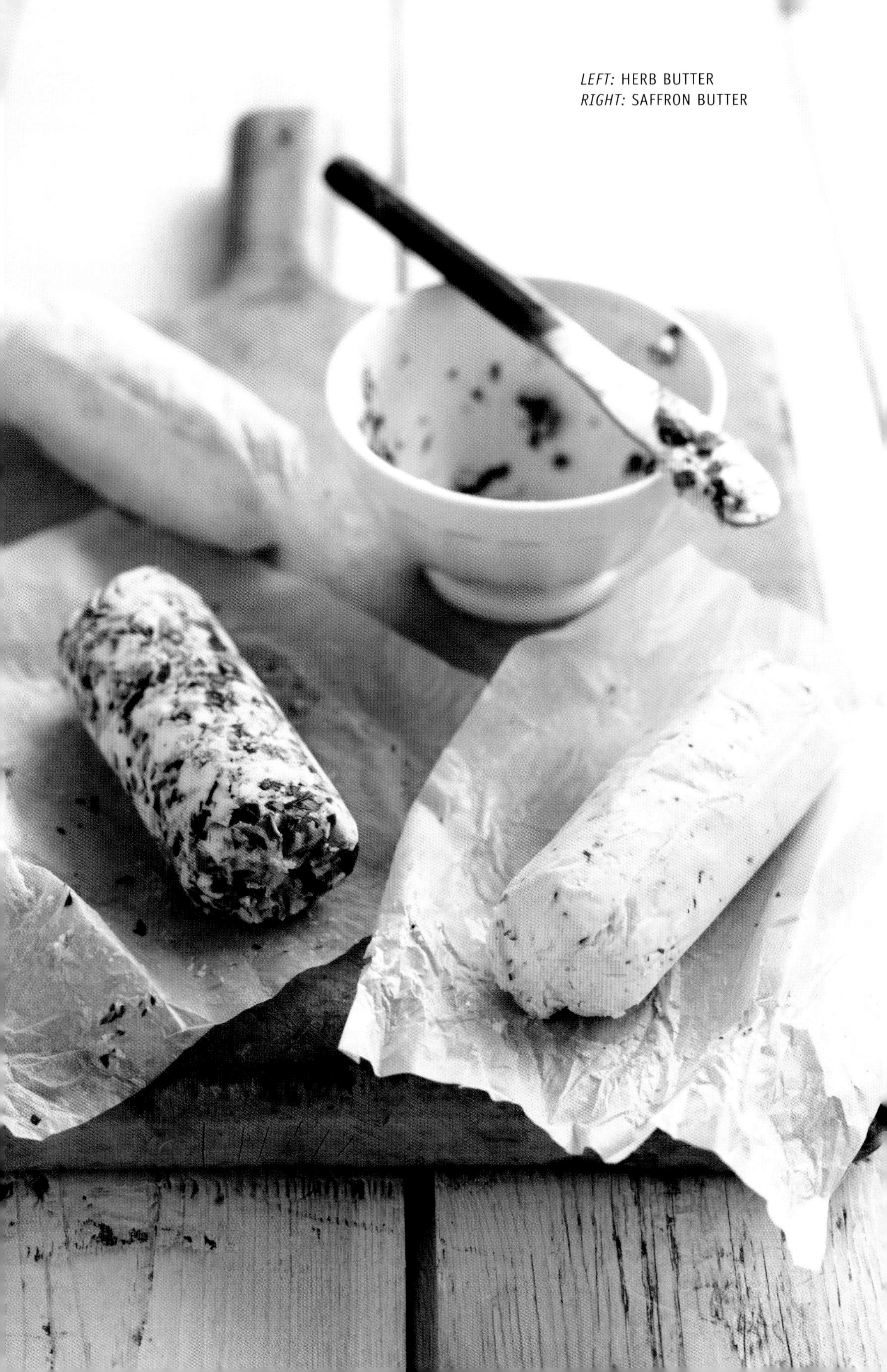

FLAVOURED BUTTERS

Flavouring butter with herbs, spices and aromatics provides a great staple to have on hand for a quick and simple supper dish. You can add an almost endless amount of flavourings to butter to serve with any type of meat, fish or vegetables. Below are just a few of my favourites, but experiment with flavours of your own choice. All the recipes below serve 4–6 people.

CAPER BUTTER

2 tablespoons capers in brine,
drained and dried
125 g unsalted butter, softened

1 tablespoon chopped fresh
flat leaf parsley
1 teaspoon finely grated lemon zest
freshly ground black pepper

SERVES: 4–6

Finely chop the capers and put in a bowl with the butter, parsley, lemon zest and pepper. Beat together with a fork until evenly combined. Transfer the butter to a small piece of greaseproof paper and roll into a log. Wrap the paper around the butter and twist the ends to seal. Refrigerate or freeze until required. Serve in slices.

VARIATIONS: HERB BUTTER

2 tablespoons chopped fresh herbs,
such as basil, chives, dill, mint
or parsley
sea salt and freshly ground black pepper

Beat the herbs into 125 g softened unsalted butter and season. Transfer to a small piece of greaseproof paper and continue to follow the recipe above.

SAFFRON BUTTER

a large pinch of saffron threads
1 teaspoon boiling water
sea salt and freshly ground black pepper

Soak the saffron in the boiling water for 10 minutes, then beat into 125 g softened unsalted butter and season. Transfer to a small piece of greaseproof paper and continue to follow the recipe above.

FENNEL AND ORANGE BUTTER

2 teaspoons fennel seeds
finely grated zest of 1 unwaxed orange
sea salt and freshly ground black pepper

Dry-fry the fennel seeds in a frying pan until toasted and fragrant. Leave to cool, crush lightly in a mortar and beat into 125 g softened unsalted butter with the orange zest and seasoning. Transfer to a small piece of greaseproof paper and continue to follow the recipe above.

LIME, CHILLI AND CORIANDER BUTTER

grated zest of 1 unwaxed lime
1 tablespoon chopped fresh coriander
1 large red chilli, deseeded and
finely chopped
sea salt and freshly ground black pepper

Beat the lime zest, coriander and chilli into 125 g softened unsalted butter and season. Transfer to a small piece of greaseproof paper and continue to follow the recipe above.

SAUCES FOR MEAT AND POULTRY

1   2   3

GRAVY

The best gravy is made in the roasting pan whilst the cooked meat is left to rest. Gravy should complement the meat it is served with, not overpower it, and all you need is some pan juices, a little wine (white, red or even Madeira or port) and some stock or water and you'll have a perfect, delicately flavoured sauce to enhance your Sunday roast.

cooked beef, chicken, pork
or lamb pan juices
100 ml white wine,
red wine or Madeira
175 ml Chicken or
Beef Stock *(page 10)*

SERVES: 4–6

Pour off and discard as much of the fat from the roasting pan as possible, leaving just the lovely meat juices. Put the pan over medium heat.

Add the wine and scrape the flavoursome, sticky bits from the base of the pan. Boil for 1–2 minutes, then add the stock and simmer for a further 3–4 minutes, or until slightly reduced. Strain before serving with the cooked meat.

PORT, ONION AND THYME GRAVY

This rich gravy is the perfect partner for sausage and mash.

75 g unsalted butter, chilled
and diced
2 onions, thinly sliced
1 garlic clove, peeled and crushed
1 tablespoon chopped fresh thyme
75 ml Ruby Port
500 ml Beef Stock *(page 10)*
sea salt and freshly ground
black pepper

SERVES: 4

[1] Melt 50 g of the butter in a saucepan and gently fry the onions, garlic and thyme with a little seasoning for 15–20 minutes, or until soft and lightly golden.

[2] Add the port, boil rapidly for 1 minute, then add the stock. Simmer for 10 minutes, or until reduced by half.

[3] Strain the sauce through a fine sieve and return to the pan. Reserve the onions.

[4] Simmer gently over low heat and whisk in the remaining butter a little at a time until the sauce is glossy. Return half the onions to the pan, heat and serve hot.

4

SAUSAGE AND MASH WITH
PORT, ONION AND THYME GRAVY

BREAD SAUCE

Infusing the milk with cloves and bay leaves gives this satisfying sauce a wonderfully aromatic finish. Although traditionally served with roast turkey, bread sauce is also great with roast chicken and guinea fowl.

300 ml milk
½ onion, peeled
6 whole cloves
1 fresh bay leaf
75 g day-old bread, crumbled
15 g unsalted butter
freshly grated nutmeg
sea salt and freshly ground black pepper

SERVES: 4

Pour the milk into a saucepan. Stud the onion with the cloves and add to the pan with the bay leaf and a little seasoning. Heat very gently until the milk reaches boiling point, then remove from the heat and set aside to infuse for 20 minutes.

Discard the onion and bay leaf and return the pan to the heat. Add the bread and butter and stir over low heat until the sauce thickens and becomes smooth. (You can purée the sauce with a hand blender if you prefer.) Season to taste and serve dusted with nutmeg.

CRANBERRY, PORT AND ORANGE SAUCE

Roast turkey just wouldn't be the same without a spoonful of tangy cranberry sauce. Use frozen cranberries if necessary.

500 g fresh cranberries
180 g granulated sugar
grated zest and juice of 2 oranges
125 ml Ruby Port
1 cinnamon stick, bruised

SERVES: 8

Put the cranberries, sugar, orange zest and juice, port and cinnamon in a saucepan and heat gently until the sugar dissolves. Bring to the boil and simmer gently for 20 minutes, or until the cranberries have softened. Discard the cinnamon.

Using a slotted spoon, remove half the cranberries to a bowl and set aside. Transfer the remaining contents of the pan to a food processor and process until smooth. Stir into the reserved cranberries and leave to cool.

HORSERADISH CREME FRAICHE

200 g crème fraîche
2 tablespoons freshly grated horseradish
1 teaspoon freshly squeezed lemon juice
a pinch of caster sugar
1 tablespoon snipped fresh chives
sea salt and freshly ground black pepper

SERVES: 6–8

There are some things that are meant to be together – beef and horseradish is just such a pairing. Tangy horseradish counters the richness of steak.

Put the crème fraîche in a bowl and stir in the horseradish, lemon juice, sugar and seasoning. Cover and refrigerate for 1 hour to allow the flavours to develop. Stir in the chives and serve with pan-fried steak.

NOTE: Fresh horseradish root is available from good greengrocers. It stores well – wrap it in a dark plastic bag and refrigerate for up to 3 months. Alternatively, you can buy freshly grated horseradish in jars.

CRANBERRY, PORT AND ORANGE SAUCE

GRIDDLED CHICKEN WITH ONION JAM,
CHARRED LEMONS AND ROCKET SALAD

ONION JAM

Although perfect with grilled chicken, onion jam is particularly versatile as it can be served as a chutney with cold meats and cheese, or as a sandwich filler. It keeps well in the fridge, but I doubt it will last long – it's just too moreish.

4 tablespoons extra virgin olive oil
4 onions, thinly sliced
4 fresh thyme sprigs, lightly bruised
100 g light soft brown sugar
100 ml red wine vinegar
4 tablespoons redcurrant jelly
sea salt and freshly ground black pepper

SERVES: 6–8

Heat the olive oil in a saucepan and gently fry the onions and thyme sprigs with some seasoning for 20–25 minutes, or until very soft and golden. Discard the thyme sprigs and stir in the sugar, vinegar and jelly. Simmer for 6–8 minutes, or until the sauce is thick and jam-like. Pour directly into a sterilized jar (see page 4) and leave to cool.

Note: Once opened, refrigerate the jam for up to 2 weeks.

QUINCE AIOLI

This recipe, adapted from Diana Henry's wonderful book on Mediterranean and Middle Eastern cooking, *Crazy Water, Pickled Lemons*, combines fruit with garlic and oil to make a savoury mayonnaise. Certainly intriguing, it is also totally delicious and goes extremely well with roast lamb, pork and chicken.

350 g quince, peeled, cored and chopped
1 garlic clove, peeled and crushed
½ tablespoon freshly squeezed lemon juice
1 teaspoon Dijon mustard
1 teaspoon caster sugar
100 ml olive oil
sea salt and freshly ground black pepper

SERVES: 6–8

Put the quince in a saucepan with plenty of cold water and bring to the boil. Cover and simmer gently for about 20 minutes, or until the fruit is very tender. Drain and leave to cool.

Put the quince in a food processor with the garlic, lemon juice, mustard, sugar and seasoning and process until smooth. With the motor running, gradually whiz in the olive oil until the sauce is thick and glossy. Season to taste.

SALSA VERDE

This Italian green herb sauce is tangy, with the distinctive flavours of capers and green olives. It goes particularly well with grilled lamb, but by altering the herbs used, it will complement almost anything. I like to keep a pot of salsa verde in my fridge to serve with meats, grilled fish such as tuna or swordfish, and as a sandwich spread.

25 g fresh flat leaf parsley leaves
25 g fresh herbs, such as mint, basil and chives
1 garlic clove, peeled and chopped
1 tablespoon stoned green olives
1 tablespoon capers in brine, drained and washed
2 anchovy fillets in oil, drained and chopped
1 teaspoon Dijon mustard
2 teaspoons white wine vinegar
125–150 ml extra virgin olive oil
sea salt and freshly ground black pepper

SERVES: 6–8

Put all the ingredients, except the olive oil, in a food processor and blend to form a smooth paste, or use a pestle and mortar. With the motor running, gradually whiz in the olive oil to form a sauce. Season to taste and refrigerate for up to 3 days.

2 large red peppers
2 tablespoons extra virgin olive oil
3 garlic cloves, peeled and crushed
350 g vine-ripened tomatoes, roughly chopped
2 tablespoons red wine vinegar
1 teaspoon dried oregano
½ teaspoon caster sugar
a pinch of dried chilli flakes
sea salt and freshly ground black pepper

SERVES: 4

SALSA ROSSA

This piquant Italian sauce uses char-grilled peppers, which produce a bright red colour and a wonderfully smoky flavour. It makes a great accompaniment to barbecued lamb or can be served with meaty fish, such as tuna or swordfish.

Grill or barbecue the peppers until charred all over (about 10 minutes). Seal in a plastic bag and leave to cool for 1 hour. Peel and deseed, reserving any juices, then roughly chop the flesh.

Heat the olive oil in a small saucepan and gently fry the garlic for 3 minutes. Add the peppers and their juices, the tomatoes, vinegar, oregano, sugar, chilli flakes and seasoning. Bring to the boil and simmer over medium heat for 30 minutes, or until the sauce is thick. Leave to cool slightly, then pour into a food processor and blend to form a smooth sauce. Serve at room temperature.

TOP: SALSA VERDE
BOTTOM: SALSA ROSSA

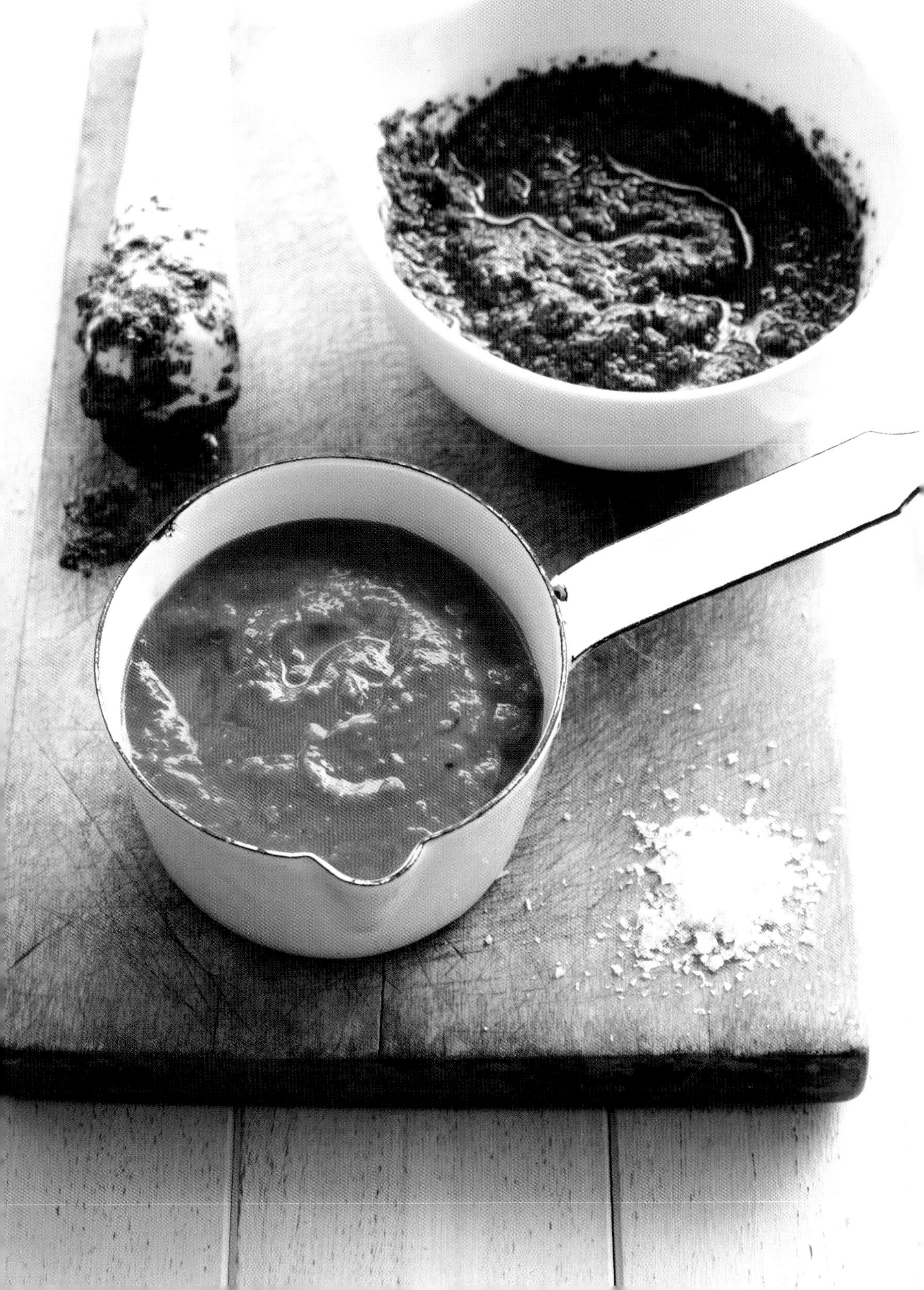

PAN-FRIED PORK CHOP WITH MARSALA SAUCE, APPLES AND SAGE

MARSALA SAUCE

Marsala is a fortified wine from Sicily that produces a sweet, herb-flavoured sauce – delicious with pork or veal.

**75 g unsalted butter, chilled
and diced
2 shallots, finely chopped
1 small garlic clove, peeled
and crushed
2 teaspoons chopped fresh sage
120 ml Marsala
150 ml Chicken Stock** (page 10)
**sea salt and freshly ground
black pepper**

SERVES: 4

Heat 25 g of the butter in a small saucepan and gently fry the shallots, garlic and sage for 5 minutes, or until softened. Add the Marsala and boil rapidly for 1–2 minutes, or until reduced by half, then add the stock and simmer gently for 5 minutes.

Strain the sauce though a fine sieve into a clean saucepan, reheat gently and gradually whisk in the remaining butter a little at a time until the sauce is thick and glossy. Serve hot.

MUSTARD SAUCE

The combination of two types of mustard gives this sauce both an intense flavour and a lovely crunchy texture. It goes perfectly with pork, but would also work well with veal or rabbit.

**four 200-g pork loin chops
25 g unsalted butter
2 tablespoons olive oil
150 ml Chicken Stock** (page 10)
**1 tablespoon Dijon mustard
1 tablespoon wholegrain mustard
100 ml double cream
sea salt and freshly ground black pepper**

SERVES: 4

Season the pork chops on both sides. Heat the butter and olive oil in a large, heavy-based frying pan. As soon as the butter stops foaming, add the pork chops and cook for 3–4 minutes on each side, or until browned and cooked through. Transfer the pork to a plate and keep warm.

Pour the stock into the pan, scraping any meaty bits from the base. Bring to the boil, add both mustards and simmer gently for 3–4 minutes. Slowly whisk in the cream and simmer for a further 2–3 minutes. Return the pork to the pan, coat with sauce and serve hot.

500 g purple plums, halved and stoned

250 ml Chinese rice wine

2 tablespoons rice vinegar

2 tablespoons clear honey

2 tablespoons dark soy sauce

½–1 teaspoon hot chilli sauce

MAKES: APPROXIMATELY 300 ML

FRESH PLUM SAUCE

This classic Chinese sauce is surprisingly simple to make and tastes really fresh and wonderful. It is great served with all types of duck dishes, including Peking duck.

Put the plums, rice wine and vinegar in a saucepan and bring to the boil. Cover and simmer gently for 20 minutes.

Mash the plums, then press through a fine sieve into a clean saucepan. Add the honey, soy sauce and chilli sauce, bring to the boil and simmer for 15–20 minutes, or until the sauce is thickened and syrupy. Pour into a sterilized bottle (see page 4), leave to cool and seal. Refrigerate for up to 2 weeks.

SOUR CHERRY SAUCE

Sour cherries are more commonly sold dried than fresh and are available from specialist food stores and health food shops. Here they are combined with both eastern and western flavours to make a delicious sauce to serve with duck or venison.

Put the ginger syrup, balsamic vinegar, cherries, wine and cinnamon stick in a saucepan, bring to the boil and simmer gently for 6–10 minutes, or until the sauce is thick and syrupy.

Discard the cinnamon, remove the pan from the heat and stir in the soy sauce and diced ginger. Serve hot.

1 tablespoon diced stem ginger, plus 2 tablespoons of the syrup

3 tablespoons balsamic vinegar

100 g dried sour cherries

175 ml fruity red wine

1 cinnamon stick, bruised

1 tablespoon dark soy sauce

SERVES: 4

PEKING DUCK IN PANCAKES WITH FRESH PLUM SAUCE, CUCUMBER AND SPRING ONIONS

BARBECUED RACK OF PORK SPARE RIBS WITH BARBECUE SAUCE

BARBECUE SAUCE

A good barbecue sauce should be tangy, smoky and rich just like this one. Serve in burgers or with barbecued beef, lamb or chicken.

200 ml passata
100 ml maple syrup
50 ml black treacle
50 ml tomato ketchup
50 ml malt vinegar
3 tablespoons Worcestershire sauce
1 tablespoon Dijon mustard
1 teaspoon garlic powder
a pinch of smoked paprika
sea salt and freshly ground black pepper

MAKES: APPROXIMATELY 400 ML

Put all the ingredients in a small saucepan, bring to the boil and simmer gently for 10–15 minutes, or until reduced slightly, and thickened. Season to taste. Pour into a sterilized bottle (see page 4) and refrigerate for up to 2 weeks.

PIRI-PIRI SAUCE

Piri-piri is a condiment used in Portuguese cooking. It was introduced into Africa by the Portuguese, hence its Swahili name which translates as 'chilli' (or 'chilli-chilli'). It is lovely drizzled over barbecued chicken, but is also wonderful with char-grilled squid or prawns.

8 red bird's-eye chillies
300 ml extra virgin olive oil
1 tablespoon white wine vinegar
a pinch of sea salt

MAKES: APPROXIMATELY 300 ML

Finely chop the chillies (including the seeds) and put in a bowl. Add the olive oil, vinegar and salt. Transfer to a sterilized bottle (see page 4) and store in a cool place for up to 1 week.

GREEN CURRY SAUCE

To make a proper Thai green curry the green curry paste must be authentic. Although you can buy ready-made green curry paste from supermarkets, it is not always that good. The one below is simple to make and will keep well in the fridge for several weeks. Add diced chicken breast and vegetables (such as those pictured) to the finished sauce and simmer for 10–15 minutes until tender.

1

600 ml coconut milk
3 tablespoons Green Curry Paste
600 ml Vegetable Stock *(page 12)*
6 large Kaffir lime leaves, torn
2 tablespoons Thai fish sauce
2 teaspoons grated palm sugar
freshly squeezed juice of ½ lime

GREEN CURRY PASTE

1 teaspoon coriander seeds
½ teaspoon cumin seeds
6 white peppercorns
3 large green chillies, deseeded and chopped
4 green bird's-eye chillies, chopped
4 spring onions, chopped
4 garlic cloves, peeled
2.5 cm galangal, peeled and sliced
4 fresh coriander stalks, roots included, chopped
1 lemongrass stalk, trimmed
2 teaspoons shrimp paste
4 teaspoons peanut oil

SERVES: 4

[1] To make the green curry paste, dry-fry the coriander seeds, cumin seeds and peppercorns until they turn golden and begin to release their aroma. Leave to cool, then grind to a powder in a spice grinder.

[2] Put all the chillies, the spring onions, garlic, galangal, fresh coriander, lemongrass, shrimp paste and peanut oil in a food processor and process to form a smooth paste. Transfer to a bowl and stir in the ground spices.

[3] To make the curry sauce, put 125 ml of the coconut milk in a wok and boil until it splits and separates into oil and milk solids. Add the freshly made curry paste and cook for about 1 minute, or until fragrant. Add the remaining coconut milk, the stock, lime leaves, fish sauce, sugar and lime juice and bring to the boil, then simmer gently for 5 minutes.

2
3

CHICKEN, COURGETTES AND PEA AUBERGINES
WITH GREEN CURRY SAUCE, CORIANDER AND
SHREDDED KAFFIR LIME LEAVES

SAUCES FOR FISH

PAN-FRIED COD WITH BUTTER AND CAPER SAUCE

125 g unsalted butter
4 tablespoons capers in brine, drained and roughly chopped
1 tablespoon freshly squeezed lemon juice
1 tablespoon chopped fresh flat leaf parsley
sea salt and freshly ground black pepper

Serves: 4

BUTTER AND CAPER SAUCE

This tangy lemon and caper butter sauce is typically served with grilled or pan-fried sole, plaice or brill but it is equally well suited to cod.

Melt the butter in a small frying pan until it turns a light golden brown. Add the remaining ingredients, stir and remove from the heat. Season to taste.

GRILLED PEPPER BUTTER SAUCE

1 large red pepper
75 g unsalted butter, diced
1 tablespoon freshly squeezed lime juice
a pinch of saffron threads
a pinch of cayenne pepper
sea salt and freshly ground black pepper

Serves: 4

Grilling the pepper until the skin chars and blackens not only makes it easier to peel, it also gives it a gorgeous smoky flavour. This sauce goes well with pan-fried cod or halibut, or with chicken.

Preheat the grill to high.

Grill the red pepper for 8–10 minutes, or until tender and charred all over. Seal in a plastic bag and leave until cool enough to handle.

Skin and deseed the pepper, chop the flesh and put in a saucepan with the butter, lime juice, saffron and cayenne. Heat through until the butter has melted.

Using a food processor or hand blender, process the pepper mixture until smooth. Season to taste and heat through. Serve hot.

CHILLI JAM

This fiery jam is a really useful ingredient to have in your storecupboard and it is so much better than the shop-bought varieties. It is hot, but the sweetness tempers this beautifully. It will store for a long time although mine never lasts very long because it's just too good. Serve with Thai fish cakes, grilled prawns, or as a sandwich filler.

500 g ripe tomatoes, roughly chopped
4 red bird's-eye chillies, roughly chopped
2 garlic cloves, peeled
1 teaspoon grated fresh ginger
2 tablespoons light soy sauce
200 g grated palm sugar
75 ml white wine vinegar
½ teaspoon sea salt

MAKES: APPROXIMATELY 300 ML

Put the tomatoes, chillies and garlic in a food processor and process until quite smooth. Transfer to a saucepan and add the remaining ingredients. Bring to the boil and simmer gently, stirring occasionally, for 30–40 minutes, or until thick and jam-like.

Spoon into a sterilized bottle or jar (see page 4) and leave to cool, then seal. Refrigerate once opened.

CHILLI CARAMEL SAUCE

The palm sugar, fish sauce and lime juice in this sauce provide that deliciously sweet, salty, sour flavour so typical of Southeast Asian cooking. The heat from the chilli makes this the perfect accompaniment to char-grilled salmon and tuna.

1 tablespoon peanut oil
2 large red chillies, deseeded and thinly sliced
2 large garlic cloves, peeled and sliced
2.5 cm fresh ginger, peeled and grated
grated zest of 2 unwaxed limes
4 tablespoons grated palm sugar
2 tablespoons Thai fish sauce
freshly squeezed juice of 1 lime

SERVES: 4

Heat the peanut oil in a small frying pan and gently fry the chillies, garlic, ginger and lime zest for 3–4 minutes, or until soft and lightly golden. Add the sugar, 3 tablespoons water, the fish sauce and lime juice and heat gently until the sugar has dissolved. Increase the heat and simmer for 5 minutes, or until the sauce is syrupy. Leave to cool for 5 minutes before serving.

BALSAMIC GLAZE

It is hard to imagine that something so simple can produce a sauce that is so versatile and useful in the kitchen. I for one always have a bottle of balsamic glaze at hand to drizzle over any char-grilled fish or chicken, add to a simple leaf salad or combine with good-quality extra virgin olive oil as a dip for crusty bread. I first tried this method of reducing cheap balsamic vinegar in order to produce something resembling the expensive, aged variety several years ago and have continued to do so regularly. It may seem extravagant to start with 500 ml, only to be left with 125 ml at the end, but believe me, it really is worth it.

a 500-ml bottle balsamic vinegar

MAKES: APPROXIMATELY 125 ML

Pour the vinegar into a small saucepan and boil gently until it is reduced by about two-thirds and reaches the consistency of a thick syrup. Pour straight into a sterilized bottle or jar (see page 4) and leave to cool. Seal and store in a cool place.

BLACK BEAN SAUCE

Dried, fermented black beans are available in packets or tinned in brine from Asian supermarkets. You will need to soak the dried beans in water for 10 minutes to remove some of the excess saltiness before use. Spoon the finished black bean sauce over pan-fried scallops or as a sauce for wok-fried mud crab.

Soak the black beans in cold water for 10 minutes, drain well and set aside.

Heat the peanut oil in a small saucepan and gently fry the garlic, chilli and ginger for 2–3 minutes, or until softened. Add the beans, stock, *kecap manis*, vinegar and oyster sauce and bring to the boil. Simmer gently for 5 minutes.

Blend the cornflour with 1 tablespoon water until smooth and stir in 1 tablespoon of the black bean sauce. Stir the mixture back into the saucepan and simmer, stirring for a further minute until thickened. Serve hot.

25 g dried, fermented black beans
1 tablespoon peanut oil
1 garlic clove, peeled and crushed
1 red bird's-eye chilli, deseeded and finely chopped
1 teaspoon grated fresh ginger
200 ml Vegetable Stock *(page 12)*
2 tablespoons *kecap manis* (sweet Indonesian soy sauce)
½ tablespoon black vinegar or rice wine vinegar
1 teaspoon oyster sauce
1 teaspoon cornflour

Serves: 4–6

---

300 ml coconut milk
250 ml Fish Stock *(page 12)*
1 red bird's-eye chilli, bruised
2 garlic cloves, peeled and bruised
2 slices of fresh ginger
8 large Kaffir lime leaves, shredded
1 lemongrass stalk, roughly chopped
½ bunch of fresh coriander stalks, roots included
1 tablespoon Thai fish sauce
freshly squeezed juice of ½ lime

Serves: 4

COCONUT AND KAFFIR LIME SAUCE

This fragrant sauce is made by simmering coconut milk and stock with herbs, spices and aromatics. As the sauce reduces and thickens, the flavours become more defined. It makes the perfect sauce to serve with steamed mussels or clams, as well as chicken.

Put the coconut milk, stock, chilli, garlic, ginger, lime leaves, lemongrass and coriander in a saucepan and bring to a very gentle boil. Simmer for 20 minutes, or until the sauce is reduced slightly, skimming the surface to remove any scum.

Strain the coconut mixture through a fine sieve, pressing it through with a wooden spoon. Add the fish sauce and lime juice to taste, and serve hot.

PAN-PRIED SWORDFISH
WITH AGRODOLCE SAUCE

PRESERVED LEMON SALSA

Preserving lemons in salt is a practice commonly found throughout North Africa, southern Italy and Middle Eastern countries where lemons grow abundantly. The salty-sharp flavour is slightly unusual but lovely. Serve the salsa with char-grilled scallops or prawns or try it with barbecued chicken.

50 g preserved lemon, diced
50 g semi-dried tomatoes, diced
2 spring onions, finely chopped
1 tablespoon chopped fresh coriander
4 tablespoons extra virgin olive oil
sea salt and freshly ground black pepper

SERVES: 4

Combine all the ingredients in a bowl and set aside to infuse for 30 minutes. Season to taste.

AGRODOLCE SAUCE

This sauce is typical of many from southern Sicily, where sultanas and capers are added to a tomato base to produce a lovely sweet and savoury flavour. It is great served with fish such as tuna, mackerel or swordfish.

3 tablespoons extra virgin olive oil
2 garlic cloves, peeled and finely chopped
grated zest of 1 unwaxed lemon
a pinch of dried chilli flakes
500 g ripe tomatoes, skinned and chopped
2 anchovy fillets in oil, drained and chopped
2 tablespoons capers in brine, drained

50 g sultanas
2 teaspoons red wine vinegar
1 teaspoon caster sugar
25 g pine nuts, toasted
1 tablespoon chopped fresh flat leaf parsley
sea salt and freshly ground black pepper

SERVES: 4

Heat the olive oil in a saucepan and gently fry the garlic, lemon zest and chilli flakes with a little seasoning for 2–3 minutes, or until soft but not browned. Add the tomatoes, anchovies, capers, sultanas, vinegar and sugar and heat gently, partially covered, for 3–4 minutes, or until the tomatoes have softened.

Stir in the pine nuts and parsley and season to taste. Serve hot.

TOP: DEEP-FRIED SQUID WITH TARTARE SAUCE
MIDDLE: PRAWNS WITH COCKTAIL SAUCE
BOTTOM: SMOKED SALMON WITH MUSTARD AND DILL SAUCE

TARTARE SAUCE

Fish and chips would not be the same without a bowl of tartare sauce – make it fresh and enjoy it with any seafood.

½ **quantity Mayonnaise** *(page 20)*
1 tablespoon finely chopped spring onion
1 tablespoon capers in brine, drained and chopped
1 tablespoon finely chopped gherkin
1 tablespoon chopped fresh flat leaf parsley
½ **tablespoon chopped fresh dill**
½ **tablespoon snipped fresh chives**
sea salt and freshly ground black pepper

Combine all the ingredients in a bowl and season to taste.

SERVES: 4

REALLY GREAT COCKTAIL SAUCE

It may well be a '70s food icon but prawn cocktail (a good one anyway) will always be a trusty favourite, because when prawns are served with crisp, shredded lettuce and coated with a tangy, creamy cocktail sauce, they are truly delicious. This version has a special ingredient, vodka, to add a little kick.

125 ml Mayonnaise *(page 20)*
1½ **tablespoons tomato ketchup**
1 teaspoon Worcestershire sauce
1 teaspoon vodka
a few drops of Tabasco sauce
sea salt and freshly ground black pepper
paprika, to garnish

SERVES: 4

Combine all the ingredients in a bowl, cover and set aside to infuse for 30 minutes. Serve garnished with a little paprika.

MUSTARD AND DILL SAUCE

This sauce is traditionally served with *gravadlax*, the Scandinavian cured salmon, served in wafer-thin slices. However, it is a delicious sauce to serve with various fish, especially any type of smoked fish.

1½ **tablespoons Dijon mustard**
1 egg yolk
1½ **teaspoons caster sugar**
125 ml sunflower oil
2 teaspoons white wine vinegar
1 tablespoon chopped fresh dill
½ **tablespoon wholegrain mustard**
sea salt and freshly ground black pepper

Put the Dijon mustard, egg yolk, sugar and some seasoning in a bowl and whisk until pale. Gradually whisk in the sunflower oil a little at a time until thickened. Stir in the vinegar, dill and wholegrain mustard and season to taste.

SERVES: 4

WATERCRESS SAUCE

A simple, pretty sauce that is perfect with pan-fried cod or other white fish.

Discard the thick stalks from the watercress and finely chop the leaves. Melt the butter in a saucepan, add the watercress leaves and sauté gently for 30 seconds, or until wilted. Add the cream and stock and simmer gently for 2–3 minutes. Liquidize in a blender to form a speckled green sauce. Heat through and serve hot.

75 g watercress
25 g unsalted butter
150 ml double cream
75 ml **Fish Stock** *(page 12)*
sea salt and freshly ground black pepper

Serves: 4

PARSLEY SAUCE

This is a modern adaptation of parsley sauce, originally made using a roux base. This lighter version is more in tune with today's tastes and is wonderful with poached, steamed or baked fish.

Bring a saucepan of lightly salted water to a rolling boil and blanch the parsley leaves for 30 seconds. Drain and immediately refresh under cold water. Squeeze out as much excess water as possible and set aside.

Heat the butter and cream together in a saucepan until the butter has melted, then boil for 1 minute. Transfer to a blender with the parsley leaves and blend until very smooth and green. Season to taste. Heat through and serve hot.

25 g fresh flat leaf parsley leaves
50 g unsalted butter
175 ml whipping cream
sea salt and freshly ground white pepper

Serves: 4

POACHED SALMON WITH PARSLEY SAUCE

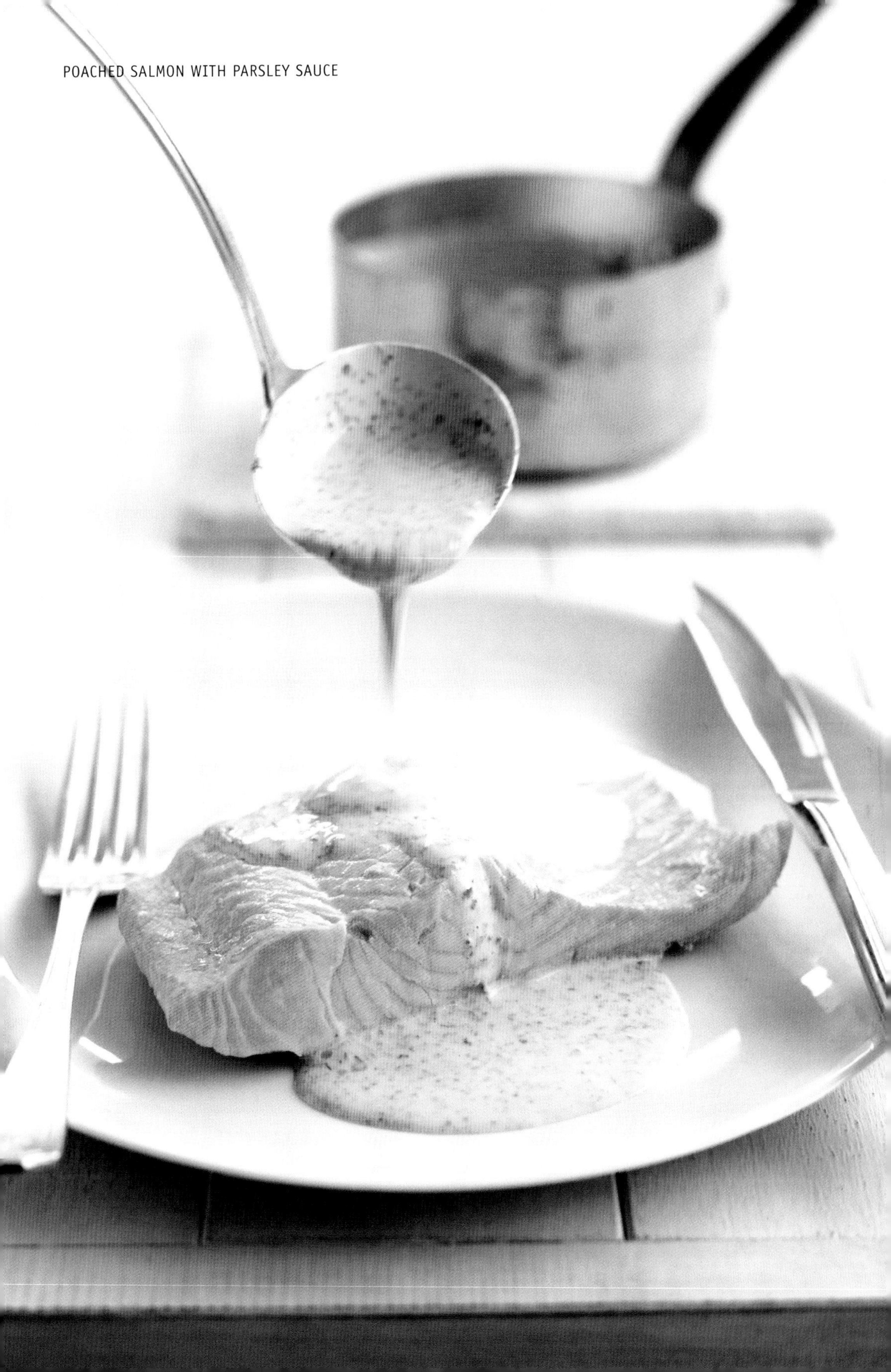

SAUCES FOR PASTA

PENNE WITH LEMON AND VERMOUTH SAUCE

LEMON AND VERMOUTH SAUCE

This is quite an unusual sauce for pasta, but no less wonderful for it. If you are unable to buy unwaxed lemons, be sure to wash the skins well before grating the zest.

finely grated zest of
2 unwaxed lemons
125 ml dry vermouth
200 ml double cream
50 g Parmesan cheese, freshly grated, plus extra to serve

2 tablespoons chopped fresh basil
sea salt and freshly ground black pepper

SERVES: 4

Put the lemon zest and vermouth in a small saucepan, bring to the boil, then simmer until the liquid is reduced by half. Leave to cool for 5 minutes.

Beat in the cream and return to the heat until warmed through. Stir in the Parmesan and basil and season to taste. Serve at once, sprinkled with extra grated Parmesan.

CHILLI, CRAB AND CREME FRAICHE SAUCE

This combination of delicate, fresh crabmeat and crème fraîche is delicious stirred into freshly cooked penne. Most good-quality fishmongers should be able to provide you with fresh crabmeat but frozen meat works equally well.

50 g unsalted butter
1 small red onion, finely chopped
2 garlic cloves, crushed
1 large red chilli, deseeded and finely chopped
500 g fresh crabmeat

200 g crème fraîche
2 tablespoons chopped fresh flat leaf parsley
fresh juice of ½ lemon
sea salt and black pepper

SERVES: 4–6

Melt the butter in a large frying pan and fry the onion, garlic and chilli for 5 minutes, or until soft but not browned.

Flake the crabmeat, making sure that there are no remaining pieces of shell. Add the crab to the pan with the crème fraîche and season to taste. Stir and heat through for a few minutes. Stir in the parsley and lemon juice. Serve hot.

BOLOGNESE SAUCE

The addition of chicken livers adds a great depth of flavour to this Italian classic. Serve over freshly cooked spaghetti or use as the base for lasagne or other baked pasta dishes.

Heat a saucepan and dry-fry the pancetta for 3–4 minutes, or until browned and the fat is rendered into the pan. Remove from the pan with a slotted spoon and set aside.

Add the olive oil to the same pan and gently fry the onion, garlic and thyme for 10 minutes, or until softened. Increase the heat, add the mince and livers and stir-fry for 5 minutes, or until browned.

Add the wine and bring to the boil, then stir in the tinned tomatoes, tomato purée, sugar, bay leaves, fried pancetta and seasoning. Cover and simmer over low heat for 1–1½ hours, or until the sauce has thickened. Discard the bay leaves and season to taste.

125 g smoked pancetta, diced

2 tablespoons extra virgin olive oil

1 large onion, finely chopped

2 garlic cloves, peeled and finely chopped

1 tablespoon chopped fresh thyme

750 g beef mince

50 g chicken livers, diced

300 ml red wine

two 400-g tins chopped tomatoes

2 tablespoons tomato purée

a pinch of caster sugar

2 fresh bay leaves (or 1 dried)

sea salt and freshly ground black pepper

SERVES: 4–6

PENNE WITH
GORGONZOLA, PECAN
AND MASCARPONE
SAUCE

25 g unsalted butter

1 garlic clove, peeled and crushed

175 g Gorgonzola cheese, crumbled

175 g mascarpone cheese

a pinch of ground mace or a little freshly grated nutmeg

100 g pecan nuts, toasted and roughly chopped

2 tablespoons snipped fresh chives

sea salt and freshly ground black pepper

SERVES: 4

GORGONZOLA, PECAN AND MASCARPONE SAUCE

The toasted pecan nuts add texture to this rich and creamy cheese sauce. Gorgonzola is a strongly flavoured blue cheese that is perfect combined with the milder mascarpone. Other blue cheeses you could use are Roquefort or even Stilton.

Melt the butter in a saucepan and gently fry the garlic over low heat for 2–3 minutes, or until soft but not browned. Stir in the Gorgonzola, mascarpone, mace and a little seasoning. Cook gently until the sauce is heated through but the cheese still has a little texture.

Remove the pan from the heat and stir in the pecan nuts and chives. Season to taste and serve hot.

125 g walnut pieces

75 g day-old white bread, without crusts

125 ml milk

1 garlic clove, peeled and crushed

25 g Parmesan cheese, freshly grated

a little freshly grated nutmeg

3 tablespoons walnut oil

4 tablespoons double cream

sea salt and freshly ground black pepper

chopped fresh flat leaf parsley, to garnish

SERVES: 4

WALNUT SAUCE

This unusual sauce from Liguria, northern Italy, is made with ground walnuts. It makes a hearty winter pasta dish.

Preheat the oven to 200°C (400°F) Gas 6.

Put the walnuts on a baking sheet and roast in the oven for 6–8 minutes, or until golden. Leave to cool. Meanwhile, soak the bread in the milk for 10 minutes, or until all the milk has been absorbed.

Put the walnuts, soaked bread, garlic, Parmesan, nutmeg and seasoning in a food processor and process until finely ground, then gradually whiz in the walnut oil to form a paste.

Transfer the sauce to a bowl and stir in the cream. Season to taste and stir into freshly cooked pasta. Serve garnished with chopped fresh parsley.

125 g niçoise olives, stoned

2 anchovy fillets in oil, drained

2 garlic cloves, peeled and crushed

2 tablespoons capers in brine, drained and rinsed

1 teaspoon Dijon mustard

4 tablespoons extra virgin olive oil

a squeeze of fresh lemon juice

freshly ground black pepper

MAKES: APPROXIMATELY 150 ML

TAPENADE

Using niçoise olives will give the finished sauce a truly authentic flavour. It is preferable to buy whole olives and stone them yourself – to do this simply press down firmly on the olives using your thumb and the olive flesh will split to reveal the stone, which is then discarded.

Put the olives, anchovies, garlic, capers and mustard in a mortar (or food processor) and pound to form a fairly smooth paste. Gradually blend in the olive oil and add lemon juice and pepper to taste.

Transfer to a dish, cover and refrigerate for up to 5 days.

PESTO

Over the past 20 years, this thick, aromatic herb and nut sauce from Genoa has travelled widely and is now used by cooks throughout the world to serve with pasta or grilled fish, or be stirred into vegetable soup. Once made, cover the surface with a little extra olive oil, seal in a container and refrigerate for up to 3 days.

50 g fresh basil leaves

1 garlic clove, peeled and crushed

2 tablespoons pine nuts

a pinch of sea salt

6–8 tablespoons extra virgin olive oil

2 tablespoons freshly grated Parmesan cheese

freshly ground black pepper

MAKES: APPROXIMATELY 150 ML

Put the basil, garlic, pine nuts and salt in a mortar and pound to form a fairly smooth paste. Add the olive oil slowly until you reach a texture that is soft but not runny. Add the Parmesan and pepper to taste. Cover the surface with a little olive oil and refrigerate for up to 3 days.

TIP: You can make this sauce in a food processor, but do not over-process otherwise the sauce will become too smooth.

LEFT: PESTO
RIGHT: TAPENADE

FOAMING SAGE BUTTER

FOAMING SAGE BUTTER

This is so simple, yet totally delicious – melted butter is sautéed until golden and nutty then mixed with fresh sage leaves and a little crushed garlic. It is particularly good with pumpkin ravioli, spinach and ricotta gnocchi, seared swordfish, or simply with plain noodles.

125 g unsalted butter
2 tablespoons chopped fresh sage
2 garlic cloves, peeled and crushed
sea salt and freshly ground black pepper

SERVES: 2

Melt the butter in a small frying pan, then cook over medium heat for 3–4 minutes until it turns golden brown. Remove the pan from the heat and add the sage leaves, garlic and a little seasoning. Leave to sizzle in the butter for 30 seconds until fragrant.

500 g butternut squash flesh, diced
1 small red onion, thinly sliced
1 tablespoon chopped fresh sage
5 tablespoons extra virgin olive oil
4 garlic cloves, peeled and finely chopped
a pinch of dried chilli flakes
50 g pine nuts
200 g feta cheese, diced
sea salt and freshly ground black pepper

SERVES: 4

ROASTED SQUASH, FETA AND SAGE SAUCE

Roasting the squash and onion first adds a slightly smoky flavour to this pasta sauce. You can use either butternut squash or pumpkin – in either case you will need a 750-g vegetable to yield 500 g flesh.

Preheat the oven to 220°C (425°F) Gas 7.

Put the squash, onion, sage, 1 tablespoon of the olive oil and some seasoning in a roasting tin, toss well and roast for 30 minutes, or until the vegetables are golden and cooked through.

Heat the remaining olive oil in a large frying pan and gently fry the garlic, chilli flakes and a little seasoning for 2–3 minutes until soft, but not browned. Add the pine nuts and stir-fry for 2–3 minutes until lightly browned. Add the roasted squash, onions, sage and the feta, and stir well until combined. Serve at once.

SEAFOOD SAUCE

This is the perfect sauce for a lavish occasion. The rich tomato *concassé* infused with saffron provides a perfect base for fresh seafood, to serve with spaghetti or linguine.

1

3 tablespoons extra virgin olive oil, plus extra to drizzle
2 garlic cloves, peeled and chopped
1 tablespoon chopped fresh thyme
625 g ripe tomatoes, skinned and finely chopped
150 ml dry white wine
150 ml Fish Stock *(page 12)*
a small pinch of saffron threads
two 350-g uncooked lobster tails
12 fresh mussels
12 large scallops
12 large uncooked tiger prawns, shelled and deveined
2 tablespoons chopped fresh basil
sea salt and freshly ground black pepper

Serves: 4

[1] Heat the olive oil in a large, wide saucepan and gently fry the garlic and thyme for 3–4 minutes, or until soft but not browned. Add the tomatoes, stir well, then pour in the wine. Bring to the boil and simmer for 1 minute, then add the stock, saffron and seasoning. Cover and simmer over low heat for 30 minutes.

[2] Meanwhile, prepare the shellfish. Cut the lobster tails lengthways down the centre of the back and discard any intestinal tract, then cut, through the shell, into 4–5 pieces. (You can leave the shell on or take it off before cooking – if you leave it on, be sure to warn guests to watch out for the shell in the sauce.) Wash the mussels in several changes of cold water, scrub the shells clean and pull out the straggly 'beard' if still attached. Cut away the tough grey muscle at the side of each scallop.

[3] Add the lobster and mussels to the tomato sauce and cook for 5 minutes, or until the mussels have opened. Discard any that remain closed. Add the prawns and cook for a further 2 minutes, then add the scallops and cook for a further minute. Remove the pan from the heat and stir in the basil. Serve hot, drizzled with extra oil.

2

3

SPAGHETTI WITH SEAFOOD SAUCE

ROASTED TOMATO SAUCE

There are few dishes more pure than a sauce made of fresh tomatoes enhanced with a little garlic, chilli, olive oil and herbs. Here I have roasted the tomatoes first to give them a really sweet flavour. This rich tomato sauce can be served with spaghetti, as part of vegetable lasagne, or as a pizza topping, as well as providing the base for soups or stews.

1 kg vine-ripened tomatoes, roughly chopped
2 tablespoons extra virgin olive oil
2 garlic cloves, peeled and crushed
grated zest of 1 unwaxed lemon
a pinch of dried chilli flakes
2 tablespoons chopped fresh basil
sea salt and freshly ground black pepper

SERVES: 4

Preheat the oven to 230°C (450°F) Gas 8.

Put the tomatoes, olive oil, garlic, lemon zest, chilli flakes and seasoning in a roasting tin in a single layer. Toss well. Roast for 45 minutes, or until the tomatoes are browned and the juices reduced to a glaze.

Transfer the tomatoes and all the pan juices to a deep bowl, add the basil and, using a hand blender, purée until smooth. Season to taste. Serve hot with some freshly cooked pasta or leave to cool in a plastic container.

Note: During the summer months, when tomatoes are plentiful and at their best, make up several quantities of this sauce and freeze for use in the winter.

CHERRY TOMATO PUTTANESCA SAUCE

4 tablespoons extra virgin olive oil
2 garlic cloves, peeled and sliced
a pinch of dried chilli flakes
500 g cherry tomatoes, halved
100 g stoned black olives, halved
6 anchovy fillets in oil, drained and chopped
4 tablespoons baby capers in brine, drained and washed
freshly squeezed juice of 1 lemon
2 tablespoons chopped fresh basil
sea salt and freshly ground black pepper
freshly grated Parmesan cheese, to serve (optional)

SERVES: 4

Puttanesca is a classic Neapolitan sauce combining olives, tomatoes, capers and anchovies. Here it is made using cherry tomatoes to add extra texture.

Heat the olive oil in a large frying pan and gently fry the garlic, chilli flakes and seasoning for 3–4 minutes, or until softened. Add the tomatoes, stir-fry for 1 minute, then stir in the olives, anchovies, capers, lemon juice and basil and heat through. Serve topped with grated Parmesan, if desired.

SAUSAGE RAGU

I have used chorizo, a spicy Spanish sausage, for this rich ragu, but you could substitute any Italian-style sausage if you prefer.

Split open the sausage skins, peel away and discard. Roughly chop the sausage meat, put in a food processor and pulse until coarsely ground.

Heat the olive oil in a saucepan and gently fry the onion, garlic, sage and seasoning over low heat for 10 minutes, or until soft and lightly golden. Add the sausage meat and stir-fry over medium heat for 5 minutes, or until browned.

Add the tinned tomatoes, wine and tomato purée, bring to the boil, cover and simmer gently for 1 hour, or until the sauce has thickened. Season to taste, stir in the parsley and serve hot.

750 g fresh spicy chorizo sausage
2 tablespoons extra virgin olive oil
1 onion, finely chopped
2 garlic cloves, peeled and crushed
2 tablespoons chopped fresh sage
two 400-g tins chopped tomatoes
125 ml red wine
2 tablespoons tomato purée
2 tablespoons chopped fresh
flat leaf parsley
sea salt and freshly ground
black pepper

SERVES: 4–6

1 kg carpetshell (vongole) clams
3 tablespoons extra virgin olive oil
2 garlic cloves, peeled and crushed
1 large red chilli, deseeded
and finely chopped
2 plum tomatoes, deseeded
and diced
75 ml dry white wine
1 tablespoon chopped fresh
flat leaf parsley
sea salt and freshly ground
black pepper

SERVES: 2

VONGOLE SAUCE

Carpetshell or vongole are tiny clams available from most good fishmongers. Use larger clams if you prefer, but vongole are particularly sweet and tender. As a last resort you can buy ready-cooked vongole in tins from Italian food stores.

Wash the clams in cold water, scrubbing any dirt from the shells, and shake dry.

Heat the olive oil in a large frying pan and gently fry the garlic and chilli with seasoning for 3–4 minutes, or until soft but not browned. Stir in the tomatoes and cook gently for 5 minutes. Add the wine and boil until reduced by half.

Add the clams and cook, covered, for 5 minutes, shaking the pan from time to time until all the shells have opened (discard any that remain closed).

Stir in the parsley and serve hot.

SAUCES FOR VEGETABLES

LEMON BEURRE BLANC

LEMON BEURRE BLANC

Here's a delicate sauce to serve with steamed green vegetables, especially tender stems of young asparagus or globe artichoke.

Put the lemon juice, wine and shallots in a saucepan, bring to the boil and cook for 2 minutes, or until the liquid is reduced to about 1 tablespoon. Add the cream and boil again until reduced to a glaze.

Reduce the heat to low. Using a balloon whisk, gradually whisk in the butter a little at a time until the sauce thickens and all the butter is incorporated. Season to taste. Strain the sauce through a fine sieve and serve hot.

3 tablespoons freshly squeezed lemon juice
3 tablespoons dry white wine
2 shallots, finely chopped
1 tablespoon double cream
250 g unsalted butter, chilled and diced
sea salt

Serves: 4

BAGNA CAUDA

Pop a dish of this warm anchovy butter in the centre of the dining table with a basket full of fresh summer vegetables and let everyone help themselves.

Heat the butter and garlic together in a small saucepan and cook very gently for 4–5 minutes, or until softened but not browned. Add the anchovies, stir well, then pour in the olive oil. Cook gently for a further 10 minutes, stirring occasionally until the sauce has softened and is almost creamy. Serve warm.

50 g unsalted butter
4 large garlic cloves, peeled and crushed
50 g anchovy fillets in oil, drained and chopped
200 ml extra virgin olive oil

Serves: 4–6

FRENCH DRESSING

This is a classic salad dressing with the perfect balance of flavours – it is neither too sharp nor too oily. It keeps for several days in a screw-top jar in the fridge. Always shake well before using.

Combine the vinegar, mustard, sugar and seasoning in a bowl and stir until smooth. Gradually whisk in the olive and sunflower oils until amalgamated. Season to taste. Store in a screw-top jar in the fridge for up to 1 week. Shake well before use.

1 tablespoon white wine vinegar
1 teaspoon Dijon mustard
a pinch of sugar
4 tablespoons extra virgin olive oil
2 tablespoons sunflower oil
sea salt and freshly ground black pepper

SERVES: 4–6

NUOC CHAM

This is a Vietnamese dipping sauce traditionally served with rice paper rolls but it can be used as a salad dressing or a dipping sauce for grilled meat and fish. It comes in various guises – with grated carrot, shrimp paste or vinegar instead of lime juice.

Put all the chillies, the garlic and salt in a mortar (or food processor) and pound to form a rough paste. Transfer to a bowl with the sugar, fish sauce and lime juice and stir until the sugar dissolves. Store in a screw-top jar in the fridge for up to 3 days.

3 large red chillies, deseeded and roughly chopped
3 red bird's-eye chillies, deseeded and roughly chopped
2 garlic cloves, peeled and chopped
a pinch of sea salt
50 g grated palm sugar
50 ml Thai fish sauce
100 ml freshly squeezed lime juice

SERVES: 4–6

JAPANESE SOY AND WASABI DRESSING

I love Japanese salad dressings where little or (often) no oil is used – they are fresh and tangy. This is a multi-purpose dressing that can be used on green salads, mixed vegetables or with seafood, especially quickly seared fresh tuna.

Combine the vinegar, mirin and sugar in a bowl and stir until the sugar dissolves. Whisk in the remaining ingredients until smooth. Store in a screw-top jar in the fridge for up to 3 days. Shake well before use.

1 tablespoon rice vinegar
1 tablespoon mirin (available from Asian food stores and health food shops)
1 teaspoon caster sugar
1 tablespoon dark soy sauce
1 teaspoon sesame oil
2 teaspoons wasabi paste
50 ml sunflower oil

SERVES: 4–6

CLOCKWISE FROM LEFT: JAPANESE SOY AND WASABI DRESSING; FRENCH DRESSING; NUOC CHAM

1 egg yolk
1 small garlic clove, peeled and crushed
2 anchovy fillets in oil, drained and chopped
1 tablespoon freshly squeezed lemon juice
1 teaspoon Worcestershire sauce
150 ml olive oil
25 g Parmesan cheese, freshly grated
sea salt and freshly ground black pepper

SERVES: 4–6

CAESAR DRESSING

It is widely agreed that Caesar Cardini, an Italian immigrant who lived in Tijuana, Mexico, invented Caesar Salad in 1924. He later moved to L.A. where he began to bottle and sell the sauce. There are many variations on the original recipe, but this is my favourite.

Whisk the egg yolk in a small bowl with the garlic, anchovies, lemon juice, Worcestershire sauce and a little seasoning until frothy. Gradually whisk in the olive oil a little at a time until thick and glossy. Add 2 tablespoons water to thin the sauce and stir in the Parmesan. Store in a screw-top jar in the fridge and use the same day. Shake well before using.

250 g Greek yoghurt
1 garlic clove, peeled and crushed
1½ tablespoons tahini
1 tablespoon freshly squeezed lemon juice
sea salt and freshly ground black pepper

SERVES: 4

TAHINI, YOGHURT AND GARLIC SAUCE

Tahini is made from ground sesame seeds and is used in eastern Mediterranean and Middle Eastern cooking. Here it helps to flavour yoghurt and results in a great accompaniment to roasted or barbecued vegetables, or grilled lamb.

Combine the yoghurt, garlic, tahini and lemon juice in a bowl and season to taste. Cover and set aside to infuse for 30 minutes before serving. Store in a screw-top jar in the fridge for up to 3 days.

PARSLEY, FETA AND PINE NUT DIP

Flat leaf parsley leaves have such a delightful flavour, they make this dip beautifully fragrant. Serve with a selection of crisp raw vegetables or as an accompaniment to grilled fish.

50 g fresh flat leaf parsley leaves
1 garlic clove, peeled and crushed
75 g pine nuts, toasted
100 g feta cheese, diced
150 ml extra virgin olive oil
freshly ground black pepper

SERVES: 6–8

Put all the ingredients in a food processor and blend to form a fairly smooth sauce. Season to taste, cover and set aside to infuse for 30 minutes before serving. Store in a screw-top jar in the fridge for up to 3 days.

PISTACHIO AND MINT SALSA

There are many adaptations of the classic basil and pine nut pesto. This one combines mint and pistachio nuts and is so versatile that it goes well with both seafood (especially grilled prawns) and roast lamb.

50 g shelled pistachio nuts
½ bunch of fresh mint leaves
1 garlic clove, peeled and crushed
2 spring onions, chopped
125 ml extra virgin olive oil
2 teaspoons white wine vinegar
sea salt and freshly ground black pepper

SERVES: 4

Put the pistachios, mint, garlic and spring onions in a food processor and process until coarsely ground. Add the olive oil and blend until fairly smooth. Stir in the vinegar and season to taste. Refrigerate for up to 5 days.

PARSLEY, FETA AND PINE NUT DIP

CARROT, ORANGE AND CUMIN DIP

CARROT, ORANGE AND CUMIN DIP

500 g carrots, chopped
2 tablespoons extra virgin olive oil
1 small onion, finely chopped
1 garlic clove, peeled and chopped
1 teaspoon ground cumin
75 ml freshly squeezed orange juice
sea salt and freshly ground black pepper

SERVES: 4–6

This is an aromatic, tangy dip perfect to serve with vegetable crudités or savoury wafers.

Steam the carrots for 15–20 minutes, or until tender. Meanwhile, heat the olive oil in a frying pan and gently fry the onion, garlic and cumin for 5 minutes, or until softened.

Transfer to a food processor, add the carrots, orange juice and seasoning and blend until smooth. Season to taste and leave to cool. Serve at room temperature. Store in a screw-top jar in the fridge for up to 2 days.

2 ripe avocados, peeled, stoned and diced
1 garlic clove, peeled and crushed
1 large red chilli, deseeded and finely chopped
2 tomatoes, skinned, deseeded and diced
2 tablespoons extra virgin olive oil
2 tablespoons chopped fresh coriander
freshly squeezed juice of ½ lime
sea salt and freshly ground black pepper

SERVES: 4–6

AVOCADO SALSA

The creaminess of avocado balances perfectly with tomatoes and the acidity of lime juice. Serve this salsa as a dip with crudités or as an accompaniment to grilled fish. To check whether the avocado is ripe, take the fruit in your hand and press gently at the neck end – if it is in peak condition, it will give a little without being too soft.

Combine all the ingredients in a bowl and season to taste. Cover and set aside to infuse for 15 minutes, then serve immediately as the salsa will start to discolour after 30 minutes.

SWEET
SAUCES

CREME ANGLAISE

Crème anglaise or custard should be stirred constantly over very gentle heat otherwise the egg yolks can curdle and spoil the sauce. It is such a versatile sauce that it goes well with a variety of hot and cold puddings – most famously with apple pie.

1

600 ml milk
1 vanilla pod, split
6 egg yolks
2 tablespoons caster sugar

SERVES: 8–10

[1] Put the milk and vanilla pod in a saucepan and set over very gentle heat until it reaches boiling point. Remove from the heat and set aside to infuse for 20 minutes, then discard the vanilla pod.

[2] Whisk the egg yolks and sugar together in a bowl until pale and creamy, then stir in the infused milk.

[3] Return to the pan and cook, stirring constantly with a wooden spoon. Do not let the sauce boil.

[4] When the mixture has thickened so that it coats the back of the spoon, remove from the heat. Serve hot, or if you prefer to serve it cold, cover the surface with clingfilm to prevent a skin forming, and leave to cool.

SABAYON

Sabayon is an emulsion, or a hot egg sauce, made by whisking egg yolks over heat to help thicken and stabilize them. Sabayon is commonly flavoured with kirsch, a cherry liqueur, but other liqueurs such as Grand Marnier or amaretto can be used. This heavenly mousse-like sauce is perfect for blanketing summer fruits.

4 egg yolks
50 g caster sugar
2 tablespoons kirsch
1 vanilla pod, split

SERVES: 4

Put the egg yolks, sugar and kirsch in a glass bowl and scrape in the seeds from the vanilla pod. Set the bowl over a pan of gently simmering water (do not let the bowl touch the water). Using an electric whisk, whisk the mixture constantly for 5–6 minutes, or until it thickens and the whisk leaves a ribbon-like trail across the surface. Serve warm.

CREME ANGLAISE

BUTTERSCOTCH SAUCE

Butter, sugar and cream combine to make
a wickedly rich toffee sauce, ideal for drizzling
over ice cream, steamed puddings and fruit.

50 g unsalted butter
175 g soft light brown sugar
2 tablespoons golden syrup
75 ml double cream
a few drops of vanilla extract

SERVES: 6–8

Melt the butter in a small saucepan. Add the sugar and syrup and
cook gently until the sugar dissolves. Stir in the cream and vanilla
extract and slowly bring to the boil. Remove from the heat and
serve hot, or leave to cool and serve at room temperature.

COCONUT CARAMEL SAUCE

Coconut milk adds an exotic twist to caramel
sauce, which makes the perfect addition to
pan-fried bananas or char-grilled mango cheeks.

100 g soft dark brown sugar
100 g unsalted butter
175 ml coconut milk

SERVES: 4

Heat all the ingredients in a small saucepan until the sugar
dissolves. Bring to the boil and simmer for 8–10 minutes,
or until the sauce is thick and glossy. Serve warm.

ROASTED PEACHES WITH BUTTERSCOTCH SAUCE

BLUEBERRY SAUCE

In this tempting sauce, fresh blueberries are simmered until they burst and release their juices and luscious flavours. Serve with cream-based puddings such as panna cotta or lemon posset.

350 g fresh blueberries
3 tablespoons caster sugar
grated zest of ½ unwaxed lemon
a squeeze of fresh lemon juice

SERVES: 4

Put the blueberries, sugar, lemon zest and 1 tablespoon water in a saucepan and heat gently until the sugar dissolves. Increase the heat slightly and simmer, partially covered, for 8–10 minutes, or until the berries soften and the sauce thickens.

Remove from the heat and add the lemon juice. Serve hot or leave to cool and serve at room temperature.

MELBA SAUCE

French chef Auguste Escoffier invented this fresh raspberry sauce in honour of the singer Dame Nellie Melba in the late nineteenth century. It was traditionally served with peaches and cream to make peach Melba, but it is equally delicious with any other fresh fruit, such as hulled strawberries or blueberries. Serve with ice cream or fruit tarts.

250 g fresh raspberries
2 tablespoons kirsch
1–2 tablespoons icing sugar

SERVES: 4–6

Put all the ingredients in a food processor and blend until smooth. Pass the purée through a fine sieve and serve.

PASSION FRUIT SAUCE

This tangy passion fruit syrup is sublime poured over lemon mousse, vanilla ice cream or fresh fruit pavlova. The sweetest, ripest passion fruit have a very dimpled skin – be sure to buy them like this.

100 g caster sugar
75 ml passion fruit pulp (from about 6 passion fruit)

SERVES: 4

Put the sugar and 100 ml water in a saucepan and heat gently until the sugar dissolves. Add the passion fruit pulp, bring to the boil, then simmer gently for 10 minutes, or until the fruit mixture is reduced slightly and has thickened. Leave to cool and serve at room temperature.

LEFT TO RIGHT: BLUEBERRY SAUCE; MELBA SAUCE; PASSION FRUIT SAUCE

KNICKERBOCKER GLORY
WITH BOTH MAPLE AND
PECAN FUDGE SAUCE,
AND CHOCOLATE SAUCE

MAPLE AND PECAN FUDGE SAUCE

This is the ultimate indulgence! Serve drizzled over vanilla ice cream or chocolate brownies.

75 g unsalted butter
75 ml maple syrup
75 ml double cream
75 g pecan nuts

SERVES: 6–8

Heat the butter, maple syrup and cream together over low heat until the butter has melted. Increase the heat and simmer fast for 5 minutes, or until the sauce is thick. Stir in the pecans and simmer for a further minute. Leave to cool for 15–20 minutes and serve warm.

Note: If you make this sauce in advance and leave it to cool completely, warm it through before serving.

CHOCOLATE SAUCE

175 ml single cream
150 g dark chocolate, chopped
15 g unsalted butter
1 tablespoon amaretto, or another liqueur of your choice

SERVES: 6–8

Use a good-quality chocolate with at least 70% cocoa solids to give a really rich, dark sauce.

Combine the cream, chocolate and butter in a bowl set over a saucepan of gently simmering water (do not let the bowl touch the water). Stir frequently until the chocolate has melted and the mixture is smooth. Remove from the heat, leave to cool for 10 minutes, then stir in the amaretto. Serve warm.

200 g white chocolate, chopped
175 ml single cream

VARIATION: **WHITE CHOCOLATE SAUCE**

Combine the chocolate and cream in a bowl set over a saucepan of gently simmering water (do not let the bowl touch the water). Stir frequently until the chocolate has melted and the mixture is smooth. Remove from the heat, leave to cool for 10 minutes and serve warm.

INDEX